D1402690

Crispus Attucks and African American Patriots of the American Revolution

Brian Siddons

NEW YORK

Published in 2016 by The Rosen Publishing Group, Inc.
29 East 21st Street, New York, NY 10010

Photo Credits: Cover American Antiquarian Society, Worcester, Massachusetts, USA/Bridgeman Images; p. 4,
7, 12, 17, 18 MPI/Archive Photos/Getty Images; p. 5 Print Collector/Hulton Archive/Getty Images; p. 8 New York
Public Library/Science Source/Getty Images; p. 9 Private Collection/Archives Charmet/Bridgeman Images; p. 11
DEA Picture Library/Getty Images; p. 13 © Boston Athenaeum, USA/Bridgeman Images; p 15 Private Collection/
Bridgeman Images; p. 16 U.S. Library of Congress; p. 19 Igor Golovniov/Shutterstock.com; p. 20 Schomburg
Center, NYPL/Art Resource; p. 21 © Nancy Carter/North Wind Picture Archives

Library of Congress Cataloging-in-Publication Data

Siddons, Brian.
Crispus Attucks and African American Patriots of the American Revolution / Brian Siddons. -- First Edition.
    pages cm. -- (Spotlight on American history)
Includes bibliographical references and index.
ISBN 978-1-4994-1741-8 (library bound) -- ISBN 978-1-4994-1739-5 (pbk.) -- ISBN 978-1-4994-1738-8 (6-
pack)
1. Attucks, Crispus, -1770--Juvenile literature. 2. Boston Massacre, 1770--Juvenile literature. 3. United States--
History--Revolution, 1775-1783--Participation, African American--Juvenile literature. 4. African American soldiers-
-History--18th century--Juvenile literature. 5. African Americans--Biography--Juvenile literature. I. Title.
E269.N3S53 2016
973.3'113092--dc23
[B]
                                        2015016287

Manufactured in the United States of America

CPSIA Compliance Information: Batch #WS15PK: For Further Information contact Rosen Publishing, New York, New York at 1-800-237-9932

CONTENTS

SLAVERY IN THE THIRTEEN COLONIES

The **slave** trade brought African slaves to North America during the 1600s, the 1700s, and briefly into the 1800s. The journey across the Atlantic Ocean was called the Middle Passage. More than 600,000 slaves were brought to the thirteen **colonies** and the United States during this period.

This image from the 1750s shows the way African slaves were treated on ships during the transatlantic crossing. Slavers thought of slaves as cargo, not as people.

This scene of an American tobacco plantation in 1725 shows male, female, and child slaves drying tobacco.

Slavery was a terrible **economic system**. The journey was horrible for the slaves. The slaves were forced to work in very bad conditions once they got to America. Slavery was an unjust system upon which the thirteen colonies depended. Slaves were needed to do the hard work necessary to raise and **harvest** crops in the fields.

THE COST OF WAR

The **colonists** who lived in the thirteen colonies came to North America for many reasons. Religious freedom and economic **opportunity** were two important reasons. Many people were willing to make the dangerous journey to have greater freedom to live the lives they wanted. Slaves did not have these opportunities. They were the property of their owners. The slave owners did not even consider their slaves to be human beings.

Britain had spent a lot of money defending its colonial territories during the French and Indian War. When the war ended in 1763, Britain had a lot of debts to pay. The British needed to find new ways to raise money to pay these debts. Even though American colonists fought and died for Britain in the war, King George III wanted the colonists to help pay for the war. The British **parliament** made laws to tax the colonists for important goods such as tea and sugar. The colonists were angry about these taxes. They had no voice in the British parliament. They had to suffer "taxation without representation." This meant they had no one in government to pay attention to their needs, while still paying taxes.

This engraving shows an angry group of Americans in New York in 1766. They are protesting the Stamp Act.

FREEDOM'S PROMISE

Slaves had no power over their lives. Their masters decided everything for them. If they **protested**, they could be killed. Some slaves risked their lives to escape to places that didn't allow slavery or to places where their masters couldn't find them. One such slave was Crispus Attucks.

This famous portrait of Crispus Attucks honors him as an American Revolutionary War hero. He is often called the first martyr of the American Revolution.

This 18th-century color engraving shows whaling ships at work. Whale oil was an important product. It was used in lamps at this time.

Crispus Attucks was born in 1723 in Framingham, near Boston, Massachusetts. His mother was a Native American. His father was from Africa. Because his father was a slave, Crispus Attucks was also a slave. Attucks helped his owner buy and sell cattle. Attucks had some freedom, but he did not want to remain a slave. Attucks wanted to work on ships.

In 1750, when Attucks was 27, he ran away. He went to work on a whaling ship. When the ship sailed out to sea, Attucks's owner, William Brown, could not find him. Attucks was finally free! For the next 20 years, he worked on ships as a sailor.

ANGER IN BOSTON

In the city of Boston, in the colony of Massachusetts, colonists were growing angry about the many taxes that the British parliament was forcing upon them. In 1768, the governor of Massachusetts, Francis Bernard, was very worried about colonists disobeying the tax laws. He asked the British king to send more soldiers to patrol the streets of Boston. He was afraid that the colonists were going to attack the tax collectors.

Attucks and other sailors and rope makers did not like the soldiers. When the soldiers were off duty, they worked at other jobs. One of the jobs was rope making. People started hiring the British soldiers to make rope. With jobs being taken by the soldiers, Attucks and the other American rope makers had a hard time earning money.

Other people in Boston did not like the soldiers either. Seeing the soldiers reminded the people that the British king was in charge. The soldiers bossed people around. People became angrier and angrier. Violence was soon going to break out.

Tax collectors were very unpopular in the colonies. This 1774 anti-British cartoon shows colonists attacking an English tax collector. The colonists have covered the collector with tar and feathers. This was a common form of punishment at the time.

THE BOSTON MASSACRE

On March 5, 1770, the anger that had been growing in Boston turned into violence. On this day, people started throwing snowballs at the British soldiers guarding the State House. Church bells started ringing, which caused more people to come running, thinking there was a fire.

Among those who came to the State House was Crispus Attucks. He had been working at the **docks**

This engraving of 1793 shows the Boston State House. It was built in 1713. The State House was the center of political life in the colonies.

Crispus Attucks, the First Martyr of the American Revolution, King (now State) Street, Boston. March 5th, 1770.   Page 16.

This 19th-century engraving shows the scene of the Boston Massacre. Crispus Attucks can be seen lying on the ground after being shot by British soldiers.

with other sailors. When Attucks got to the State House, the crowd was taunting the British soldiers. The soldiers were growing very nervous in front of the angry crowd. Some people in the crowd even dared the soldiers to shoot.

No one knows exactly what happened next. Some people said Attucks was holding a stick. Others said he was holding a club. Some said he struck a soldier's gun. Others said he did not hit the gun. Some people said they heard a voice yell "Fire!"

One of the soldiers fired and shot Attucks. The other soldiers began to shoot. When they stopped firing, Attucks and two other men were dead. Two more men died later from their wounds. Six other people were also hurt. After the shooting, the British soldiers left Boston.

Some people thought Attucks and his men were heroes. Others thought they were just part of a **mob**. A man named Samuel Adams wanted to use the shootings as a way to get colonists excited. Adams was a patriot. He wanted colonial independence from Britain. He wanted the colonists to get angry with the British soldiers. He was the first to call the shootings the Boston **Massacre**. He hoped to get more colonists to demand independence from Britain.

The Boston Massacre was a turning point in American history. It united many colonists against British rule. Thousands of people came to the men's funeral. They made a big **procession** to the cemetery. Stores were closed, and bells rang.

This illustration is by the famous 20th-century artist Howard Pyle. It shows Samuel Adams arguing with Governor Hutchinson after the Boston Massacre. Adams demands that British soldiers leave Boston.

THE AMERICAN REVOLUTIONARY WAR

Crispus Attucks was the first American to die in the American fight for independence. News of his death spread quickly throughout the colonies. Paul Revere made an engraving of the massacre that made colonists want to fight back against the British. The colonists feared they would be completely enslaved by British military rule.

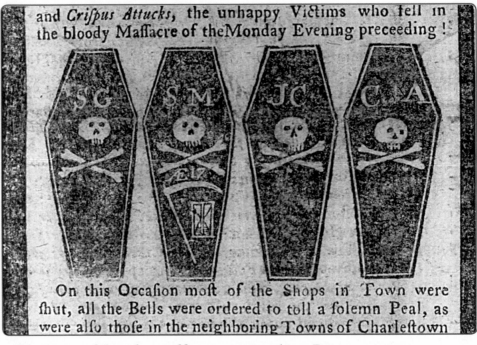

The image of these four coffins was printed in a Boston newspaper on March 12, 1770. The coffins carry the initials of the four Americans killed during the Boston Massacre.

The Boston Tea Party happened on the night of December 16, 1773. This painting, however, shows the Boston Tea Party as happening during the day.

In the next five years, there would be many more acts of protest against unfair British laws and taxes. The Boston Tea Party was one such protest. These protests showed that Americans were willing to fight against the British for their freedom.

Soon the protests turned into actual battles. The Battle of Lexington and Concord on April 19, 1775, was the first battle of the American Revolution. African Americans fought bravely alongside other patriots in this and many other battles.

AFRICAN AMERICAN PATRIOTS GO TO WAR

The African American patriots who fought in the American Revolution were fighting for two causes. One cause was freedom for the thirteen colonies from British rule. Personal freedom was another cause.

Many of the African Americans who fought were slaves. Sometimes they fought in place of their owners and died doing so. Some were promised their freedom

This 1779 illustration shows an African American soldier of the Continental army. He is using a cannon.

Contributors
To The
Cause...

U.S. 10c

Salem Poor ✾ *Gallant Soldier*

This 1975 United States ten-cent stamp was printed to celebrate the contributions of Salem Poor to the American Revolution.

if they fought. The British also offered to free any slave who fought on their side. This tactic made General George Washington recruit more African American soldiers than before. As many as 5,000 African Americans, both freemen and slaves, fought as patriots.

Salem Poor, a slave born in the late 1740s, fought bravely at the Battle of Bunker Hill. Poor won special praise from the officers who fought with him. They called him "a brave and gallant soldier." Of the thousands of colonial soldiers who fought at this battle, he is the only soldier to be praised in this way.

Peter Salem was another freed slave who fought in the Revolutionary War. Born in 1750 in Framingham, Massachusetts, Salem fought bravely at the battles of Bunker Hill, Saratoga, and Stony Point.

At the Battle of Bunker Hill, Salem is said to have fired the shot that killed British major John Pitcairn. In 1882, the town of Framingham built a monument to honor Peter Salem.

Peter Salem, the Colored American, at Bunker Hill.   Page 21.

Peter Salem fought bravely in many battles of the American Revolution. Salem's grave can be seen at the Old Burying Ground in Framingham.

This memorial is at Valley Forge, Pennsylvania. It was made to celebrate all the African American soldiers of the American Revolution who fought for freedom.

There were two military companies in the
Continental army that were made up of freed slaves.
One was called the Bucks of America. The Bucks
were from Massachusetts. The other company was
the 1st Rhode Island Regiment. The brave soldiers in
these companies helped the American colonies to win
freedom from the British.

Sadly, fighting for the freedom of the colonies
did not always bring personal freedom to African
Americans. Many African Americans still found
themselves in slavery after the Revolutionary War.
They were denied their rights, even after helping the
colonies achieve their own. African Americans still
suffered from **discrimination**.

The ideals of freedom that drove the colonists to
go to war with Britain eventually brought an end to
slavery in the northern states. Slavery continued in the
southern states, however. The United States of America
would have to fight a civil war before slavery was
abolished in the entire country.

GLOSSARY

colonies (KAH-luh-neez) Areas in new countries where large groups of people move who are still ruled by the leaders and laws of their old country.

colonists (KAH-luh-nists) People who live in colonies.

discrimination (duh-skrih-muh-NAY-shun) The act of unfairly treating a person or group of people differently from other people or groups of people.

docks (DAHKS) Places along a shore where ships can come to load and unload goods.

economic system (ehk-uh-NAH-mihk SIHS-tuhm) The system by which goods and services are produced, sold, and bought in a country or region.

harvest (HAHR-vuhst) The season when crops are gathered from the fields or the activity of gathering crops.

massacre (MAAS-uh-kuhr) The act of killing many people who do not or cannot fight back.

mob (MAHB) A crowd of people acting out of control, often damaging property or hurting other people.

opportunity (ah-puhr-TOO-nuh-tee) An amount of time or a situation in which something can be done.

parliament (PAHR-luh-muhnt) The group of people who are responsible for making the laws in some kinds of government.

procession (pruh-SEH-shun) A group of people walking in an organized way.

protested (proh-TEHST-ed) Showed or expressed strong disagreement with something.

slave (SLAYV) A person treated as property and forced to work without pay.

INDEX

PRIMARY SOURCE LIST

Page 4: Engraving, *Slave Ship* by unknown artist was published in *Life and Death on the Ocean: A Collection of Extraordinary Adventures in the Form of Personal Narratives*, by Henry Howe in 1856. Stored at the Library of Congress, Prints and Photographs Division.
Page 5: Illustration from *A Compleat History of Drugs*, by Pierre Pomet (1658–1699). He was a doctor to King Louis XIV (1638–1715). Originally published in 1694, France; English-language version in 1725, London.
Page 11: *John Malcom* by Philip Dawe. Dawe was a political artist (1750–1785). It was printed by R. Sayer & J. Bennett, Map and Printsellers of London, England, on October 24, 1774.
Page 12: *Boston State House* by unknown artist, published in *Massachusetts Magazine*, July 1793.
Page 16: This illustration appeared in *The Boston Gazette and Country Journal*, on March 12, 1770. It was created by Paul Revere, engraver (1735–1818). The letters on each coffin stand for Samuel Gray, Samuel Maverick, James Caldwell, and Crispus Attucks. It is stored at the Library of Congress.
Page 20: *Brave Colored Artillerist, Peter Salem, the Colored American at Bunker Hill* by unknown artist. This drawing was published in 1855 by R.F. Wallcut as part of a collection on African American patriots. William C. Nell was the author, with an introduction by Harriet Beecher Stowe (Author of *Uncle Tom's Cabin*). Stored at the Schomburg Center for Research in Black Culture, NYPL.

WEBSITES

Due to the changing nature of Internet links, PowerKids Press has developed an online list of websites related to the subject of this book. This site is updated regularly. Please use this link to access the list: www.powerkidslinks.com/soah/cris